A. BISSET

Always Healing Never Healed

The Shift From Chronic Healing to Evolution

To us

Contents

1

The Beginning: The Introduction

The deep relief of being healed once and for all was worth a thousand times the fear and suffering I perceived would come with it. Being responsible. Being free, finally. Ultimately, it had little to do with all of the treatments, herbs, diets, and rituals, or the tests, appointments and the enormous amount of time and energy spent on understanding my past, my medical and psychological history and symptom analysis. No matter how holistic or mainstream the approach, it wasn't really about any of that. In the end it came down to a simple shift, in attention.

Before you throw this book in the trash, let me explain and also empathize wholeheartedly. The simple shift required nothing but a decision and a subsequent action, but it took me years of work to see this, accept it, reject it, and do it all over again many times until the moment I finally just did it and that was that. I know now that none of it was necessary, but also, perhaps it was, because that's the way it eventually happened. Struggle means something very different to me now and likely it was a necessary training after all for what came after the healing.

So if you've suffered greatly on your healing process so far, it certainly was not in vain. The focus isn't on the process anymore though. This won't be another system or therapy for drawing connections about what happened to you, analyzing your neuroses, seeking out unidentified trauma or diagnosing new illnesses to explain symptoms and lead you towards yet another protocol or healing modality. Your future is much, much more interesting than that. As attractive as healing can be when we are unwell, your future has no further healing, potentially. And at risk of sounding like a pyramid scheme- life coach-salesman, you *can* do it, it's in your hands, and it's available right now. Truly.

I am not the originator of this idea but rather a distiller and translator of treasured material by my own mentors, who pulled out the crucial messages from *their* own teachers and professional experience. After reading their work it was clear to me how much of it overlapped, and the truth they all expressed in different terms. While I'd love everyone to read all of their content, many won't. So this small book is a peak into it. And perhaps it is all that is needed. For practitioners or anyone in a similar role, the reading list may be of use. It is in our best interest as health-care providers and mental health practitioners to make this shift in our own attention. To place our awareness on the part of us and our patients that is healed, whole, unbroken, and not to perpetuate the chronic healing state of those in our care, even whilst we assist with addressing the ailments of the body. I have been drawn to certain mentors for their vast life and clinical experience as well as ability to convey concepts beautifully using words. Sometimes much better than I can, and in those instances I have provided direct quotes.

What we can learn from them is that the process of *always* healing ultimately prevents us from living a life of meaning. It creates a perpetual loop of chronic stress that continually weakens us, further substantiating our need for more time for healing, and in turn creating more illness, more suffering… and the loop continues.

Jungian analyst James Hollis describes the pivot, from healing to evolution, as the transition between the first and second halves of our lives, psychologically. He says of this that,

> *"For those willing to stand in the heat of this transformational fire, the second half of life provides a shot at getting themselves back again. They might still fondly gaze at the old world, but they risk engaging a larger world, one more complex, less safe, more challenging, the one that is already irresistibly hurtling toward them".* [1]

There is a choice to be made. In this book may be a moment that serves as a catalyst for the decision that will shift you from always healing to truly healed, forever, with no more time needed. The false is removed and we are left with only the True, the Good, and the Beautiful. The entire journey to this moment is left far in the distant past as you forge your very meaningful future. [2]

Regardless of age, whatever extent of life we have left is often allocated to overcoming that part of life already lived.

-Lonny Jarrett [3]

2

The Adaptations: Necessary and Destructive

For most of us, something happens to us that changes our view of the world for the first time. Usually it's in early childhood, likely before we even remember. We have an understanding about how the world works, how safe and healthy we are, and how people should treat us. Then something happens. A medical emergency, an altercation between family members, a loss, a betrayal of trust, or other harm. With our development up to that point, our understanding of language, our meaning-making abilities, we form a conclusion about that event that helps us understand it in the context we have as a child. Making sense of things helps us explain to our young selves why it happened, and what we need to do in order to protect ourselves going forward. In some cases, it may be for literal survival. In others, emotional and psychological resilience. We are so incredibly open, vulnerable and malleable at that stage. We simply adapt.

It is difficult to pinpoint what may have happened from our adult perspective as there needn't have been anything that seems obviously traumatic. In fact, it may have been something totally benign. Rather than the event itself causing direct harm, it is *the relationship we have to the event* that can create the real, and potentially lasting, damage.

* * *

When I was two and a half my parents divorced. I didn't understand much about it at that point, but my older brother was nearly five and my parents explained to him that in 6 months they would be separating. They did their best to reassure him that it was no fault of his. While he understood that he had not caused this, what he didn't understand in his young mind was what a 'divorce' actually was. Somewhere along the way he gathered that it meant he would be put up for adoption at this 6 month mark. My parents had no idea of course and no opportunity to know either. Every few weeks or so he would nervously ask, 'how long until the 6 months is over?' and they would let him know and again, reassure him about how much they loved him and that it wasn't his fault. For 6 months this five year old held so much sadness about the end of his time with his parents. When the time came for the final divorce and the move out of the house, he broke down in tears and said his goodbyes to them. Luckily at this point, through some questions and answers, my mom figured out what happened and corrected his understanding. While the divorce itself ended up being very amicable, it is the conclusions my brother's young self made that were so *potentially* traumatic. Luckily he had an opportunity to gain more context that he could make sense of at his age.

But in a similar situation unbeknownst to the parents, a child may develop any number of adaptations. They may create beliefs, and later behaviors, that protect them from the pain they endured or that they anticipate they will experience in the future. These adaptations help immensely for them to get through these events. But over time, the adaptations remain while the circumstances change, and eventually they become less useful, and even destructive.

***

When we ask the question, 'How did we come to be who we think we are?' a significant part of the answer is found in the conscious, learned influences of our family and the environment we were born into, but much more of our lives will be deeply governed by the powerful patterns we adopted in order to survive in the larger world. These instruments of adaptation allowed survival, for which we are grateful, but their autonomy in our lives binds us to a disempowered past and the cycle of repetition. We are summoned to leave them behind and endure the anxiety that always accompanies transcending the predictable securities of the past.

-James Hollis [4]

For example, if a young child loses someone close to them, they may create adaptations that help them cope with their sadness. They may become very adept at distracting themselves from feeling pain, and numbing themselves out. This helps them survive the loss. They may even go so far as to avoid developing feelings of love again, as a protection from enduring loss in the future. This is very effective until they grow up and spend most of their lives avoiding pain or worse, love and connected. They may be unable to form meaningful relationships and end up isolated and depressed. Their ability to numb may protect them from feeling enough pain to hit a turning point and realize what has happened. And so it may perpetuate for a lifetime. Naturally, it would bring great anxiety to anticipate relinquishing these adaptations and being left raw to the experience of pain.

We can look at it through physical adaptations as well. When there is mechanical damage or physical trauma to a muscle, our brain senses an issue and shuts off that muscle, much like a circuit breaker in our house. This protects it from continuing to fire in a harmful way, which would create more inflammation and damage to the injured site beyond the initial reaction and protection. This is quite helpful in order to allow the area to heal and mitigate further harm. With that muscle switched off, other muscles and soft tissue have to adapt in order to continue stabilizing joints and continuing movement. Alternatively, movement is avoided altogether.

So we adapt but it's also a maladaptation. These other tissues can substitute but they still have to do their normal job, so they can only do this adaptation for so long before they start to fatigue and become injured or inflamed. Things seem to go on as normal but meanwhile we're forming tight bands, knots and adhesions. We get more tense and more tired, but things are still sort of *fine*. The tension however is sending constant signals to the brain that something is not quite right. If we recognize a weakness in this area and, with good intentions, attempt to strengthen it, we only make the *mal*-adaptations work harder to compensate, making the issue even worse. It's clear now that no amount of massaging or soothing balm will correct the issues. We've got to switch the muscle back on first, and let the other muscles and tissues off the hook, and function as a full system again. This is the same as psychological therapy. If we keep trying to ease the symptoms, alleviate anxiety that has developed, or talk through the issue with the part of us that has the issue, we will never access the part of us that was shut down. In many cases, therapy will serve to reaffirm the maladaptive mechanism because it only addresses the part of the person that is maladapted, and further reinforces that part of the self, hearing it out for 50 minutes each week.

Instead of seeing these maladaptions as evidence of where we went wrong in life, I see it more as a way to understand the parts of ourselves and our behavior that seem to be hurting us, which we keep doing anyway. It's easy to feel frustrated at ourselves as though we are broken in some way, unfixable, or flawed. The necessary adaptations simply persisted beyond their context, rendering them destructive rather than protective. And yet, even after we identify them, we cling to them.

James Hollis's words are the most apt on this phenomenon.

> "After all, these adaptive stratagems experimentally evolved to help us survive, and without them we might not have gotten out of childhood. But can we readily give our lives over to these conditioned reflexes now that we know they are there? Can we abdicate adulthood because we have that archaic childhood vision of self and world to care for and defend? Go ahead, defend that child as one should, but do not give it the power of choice in your adult life.
>
> Remember that the place of origin for all these patterns is in (1) the traumatic past, (2) from the disempowered world of the child, and (3) confined within the limited range of choices and values of that world. Understandably, the internalization of these values, roles, and scenarios as the reflexive way to live a predictable, safe life once made sense, but today they condemn one to an iron wheel

of repetition. Do not judge this history, for it was as it had to be, but do not abdicate the possibility of the present either. Learn the reflexive patterns, see where they show up, what activates them, what damage is done to self or others, and learn anew that the adult can manage so much more than the child." [5]

It is worth reading a few times.

The child who created these patterns did so out of both necessity and limitations in choice and perspective. There is no fault on the child in this. The adult learning this history is not the same as the child, and new conclusions may be formed as their meaningful future is created.

For most of you who have been in a healing process, or on a 'journey' or 'path' for quite some time now, you are probably familiar with events of your past that created maladaptations. You are likely aware of destructive mechanisms playing out. You probably know all about the trauma you endured and the illnesses you've suffered. I'm sure it's not really news to you at all. And that's fine. In fact, you don't need to spend a moment more on them. No further diagnosis is needed. This isn't about understanding your protective mechanisms more deeply or further explaining your identity of being unwell. Eventually the maladaptions fail and fall apart. The compensatory muscles weaken and become injured themselves. The original muscles are forced back into action. The muscle was always there, ready to be turned back on, but our attention was in another place, on the tight bands and knots that had developed, on the anxiety and fear that protected us and kept us going just enough.

It was not the hurt muscle that really prolonged our suffering after all. That healed long ago. It was not the harmful event that occurred. We survived that. What persisted was the adaptations. The response to what happened. We created an elaborate, convincing, partially true, personal story.

The provisional personality, an interwoven fabric of adaptations, may be far removed from the inherent Self, but, "for good or ill, it brought us this far," so we are afraid to let go of it now. However, life has a way of calling this provisional personality into question. For most of us, this fated encounter is a shocking and confusing appointment.

-James Hollis [6]

3

The Story: Personal Past and Being Special

I f you were given a writing prompt that simply stated "tell your story", do you already know what you would write? Anyone who has been healing for a long time has a good idea of what their story would be. At least the question wouldn't be bewildering. Usually it is an account of *what has happened to us.* Stories might spring to mind immediately in fact, such as pivotal life events, many of them likely painful. Our suffering stands out because it's potent and remains with us for a long time. It gives some meaning to our lives. It helps us explain how we are, and why, our quirks and anxieties, our fears. The story gives us an edge too. Perhaps something happened to us that hasn't happened to a lot of people we know. It's something we survived, something we suffered. It's like a resume of things we have been through. Sure we wish they wouldn't have happened, but they also make us more interesting. Our story can prove our resilience or explain our failures.

One thing to note about stories when we are 'still healing' is that they tend to be very personal. And of course our own story is personal. It's

13

our story after all. Our story tells all about what happened to *us*. Our own trauma, our own sickness. Usually when we are unwell, our entire story becomes about being unwell. It is all about our journey of healing. When someone is healing, they will try many things in the process, anything. In fact, their whole life becomes about healing. Which is the same as saying it becomes about *being* unwell, or not yet being healed. We do not seek out healing unless we consider ourselves not yet healed. Sick, traumatized, hurt, broken, damaged. Over time this becomes who we are. We *are* healing. It's like a full-time job. It takes up expensive real-estate in our minds and internal landscape. It becomes the topic of the information we consume daily, of the conversations we have. It is the focus of others we seek out as companions, as our circle. We may join groups of others who are healing from the same trauma and spend hours talking about our healing of that trauma. We may go to appointment after appointment, treatment after treatment. Workshops, courses, protocols. Our story says we have been hurt and need healing, and all of these activities and modalities promote just that. It fits the story.

In these situations we are often given a platform. We are given attention. We get to tell our story over and over again. There may be others who also had trauma, but not like *ours*. Others may suffer from this chronic illness, but it's not as *complex*. Perhaps *we* have several illnesses. Mysterious symptoms. We are unresponsive to conventional treatment. Our situation is rare. Undiagnosable. Multiple-diagnoses. In fact, it seems that we are just so different from others, our situation is so unique, our suffering so hard to understand that we are just….special.

A mentor in Chinese Medicine, Lonny Jarrett, once spoke about patients he's had who have a story about how bad their illness is, their symptoms, their trauma. They've tried so many interventions that were fruitless, it is almost as though they are unhelpable. He asks them sometimes if they are really so bad. *Oh yes,* they say. *The worst?* He asks. *The very worst,* they say. [7]

Being the *worst* is the same as being special. The worst sets you apart from those that are simply bad, that were only somewhat hurt or broken. If you are the *most* broken, you are also the most special.

* * *

In my early twenties when I used to partake in Ayahuasca ceremonies, I had an experience that shook me deeply. I drank my portion of the tea and was having a particularly uneventful trip, or journey. I felt like I was "in", but nothing remarkable was occurring, no trips to the pyramids, no body dismemberment or visions of my ancestors. And then suddenly there was just a presence. As I understood it at the time, this was the Ayahuasca, the mother spirit of the medicine. Once I acknowledged 'her' we began having a casual conversation. At one point she paused from the small talk and said, very directly, that my message from all this was:

'you are not special'.

This took me aback. I had braced myself for receiving the cure to all illness, or the meaning of life. This message hit me quite hard. The feeling was pain. I was offended. I even felt embarrassed. It insinuated somehow that I had been believing that I *was* special, that I needed to be told otherwise. I felt ashamed and wondered if others knew. She continued, after letting me smolder in it for a few eternal moments, *you need to understand this,*

"being special is separation".

Ah. The numinous feeling returned. I understood it then. This was still some time before I got very ill, so I hadn't even formed an identity about being sick yet. But I had come to the ayahuasca ceremonies a couple of years before with the intention of being in service to the world. I felt I had something to offer, to help. I didn't think I needed to fix anything about myself. And in a big way, it was totally true, and the point of this whole book. But I also felt that I *uniquely* had something to offer. Which is also true really, for all of us. *But* I thought that I was somehow different from others. I thought that whatever set me apart was what gave me the ability to be in service. What really gave me that ability was eventually my understanding that I was actually part of everything, just like everyone else, and I was in service to the evolution of us all, not to my own validation. At that point though, my pain was still about my past, about me. The duty is not to heal that for my own story, for the conclusion. The duty is to heal it so that I can heal that small part of the whole. As long as I was special, I was separate from others, from everyone and everything. My healing was only in service to myself and my little story of pain.

I don't know anymore if I was speaking with the great mother Ayahuasca herself, or if the substance I ingested switched off my default mode network and allowed me to pay attention to parts of my consciousness that, for the sake of daily operations, I normally ignored. The rest of me. The bigger picture. The parts that weren't concerned with day-to-day survival, or the story. Accessing the whole of me showed me that this 'whole' was in fact only a particle in the bigger 'whole' of everything, and I had only been paying attention to a tiny part of the tiniest parts of myself. Not a single cell, or even an atom, or a proton, but an even tinier quark of a story. *Not* being special allowed me to instantaneously merge with all of consciousness, as woo as it sounds. My story was a shiny thread in the great web. It wasn't really personal at all. My past was part of all history and the future I was creating would be as well.

Lonny Jarrett describes this at the ground of being, the deepest ground. He says,

> *"The discovery of this deepest ground, as a dimension of the self, is radical and potentially changes everything. Having seen through the existential knot at the root of the deception that is ego, that we exist as discrete entities,* we are provided with the possibility to live for a higher purpose informed by a greater depth. *From this moment on, 'personal' experience is always* contextualized by a limitless context *that imparts a dimension of ease, a sense of mystery, and anticipation to experience".*
>
> -Lonny Jarrett [8]

After that experience, this understanding of the deepest ground that Jarrett talks about really stuck with me. But over time it faded a bit and new events happened, new pain, new illnesses, and a new story was created. It took a lot more suffering and separation to finally become not special once and for all.

In your story, are you the center of the universe,
or a naturally small, but integral part in the web that is much
greater
than your single thread?

4

The Reasons: Needing More Time

The ego deems the continued presence of unpleasant thoughts, feelings, emotions and sensations as constituting proof of not being 'there' yet, of the severity of our damage, of being 'broken', and, most importantly, of needing more time to heal. Identification with the wound is so deeply rooted that for the ego to let go of it would be to die for lack of being able to locate itself in time and space...

...Although many seem to be consuming experience under the auspices of healing, I meet relatively few who consider themselves "healed", done with the process, and ready to go, very few who are finders and no longer seekers. Many seem to be so identified with a sense of "problem" that to let go of it would leave a void. That void terrifies the ego as it projects only its own death into that empty space. Truly, many people have suffered terribly. But I've never met anyone whose past traumas, regardless of how serious they may have been, are more compelling than their future potential.

-Lonny Jarrett [9]

I f the question was posed to you, 'why not just be healed right now?', what would your initial answer be? The question could rightly be taken as a little insensitive. The asker likely hasn't been through what you've been through, nor do they understand what it's like to be sick or to have been terribly hurt, and how many things you have already tried. If you give the question the time of day, you would have many valid reasons for why you can't just *be healed* already, it's almost obvious. You might have an actual illness. You have test results and a laundry list of symptoms. You have tried the conventional medications, the alternative medicines, the meditation, the herbal protocol. You've altered your diet and lifestyle to extreme degrees. You've spent countless hours and dollars trying to get well. What is the point of a question like this? If you could be well of course you *would be.* Right?

Pose the question in a circumstance of trauma, or emotional pain, or triggers and it must come from either a place of total ignorance or it is just downright rude. Does the asker think you *want* to be like this? Do you? Do you have a choice?

The question has a different energy if it's more neutral, almost clinical. Merely another writing prompt, an organizational exercise. Let's put down the reasons that you aren't healed already, right now. And there *are* reasons of course, otherwise the healing would be done. So you can pause here and actually write them down on a piece of paper, or in the notes section of your phone. Or you can just take a moment and go through them in your head. Most people on a healing path are very aware of the many reasons; They are still broken, wounded. They were hurt so badly. They don't have the vast resources needed for the extreme case of their condition. They still have this or that bacteria, virus, spirochetes. They have certain genetics, or an autoimmune condition. They don't have the support they need from family or friends. They are still processing what occurred. They lived in a moldy house. They keep getting hurt by others. There is no known cure. There is not even a diagnosis. There are multiple diagnoses.The medicine doesn't work for them. They haven't finished this protocol yet. There is another layer to uncover. They haven't dealt with everything that happened in the past. There is more they have forgotten, suppressed….

These are just a few examples of the many reasons that we may not yet be healed. They point to one main thing.

We need more time.

We can't be healed just today, now. We aren't ready. There is more to do. It is so severe that it will take a lifetime. In fact, we may never be healed at all!

Our reasons have a nearly direct link to our story like we talked about in the last chapter. They are most certainly, almost always, very real and valid reasons for feeling how we feel, for being unwell. They are clearly there, they happened, or are still happening. Much like our story, they give us an explanation for where we are at in life. For our failures, or even just for our lack of attempt at success. After all, if we have reasons for needing more time, then how can we pursue the life of someone healed? If we have reasons to keep healing, then that becomes our occupation. That gives us purpose in life. It is like a big check box showing that we are still working on something. We're not just sitting around! We are processing!

* * *

Rickson Gracie, one of the greatest Brazilian Jiu Jitsu martial artists, wrote in his book about his fight against King Zulu in which he almost quit.

"This fight exposed me to the most primal kind of fear that comes from within. My insecure state of mind came from the fear of losing. If you fear something that has not even happened, then quitting becomes a form of self-protection. Fear is not the enemy; it's simply a self-protection mechanism that must be managed."
  -Rickson Gracie [10]

Our reasons are how we quit stepping into the ring before we even get there, claiming we are still perfecting our training, or healing an injury.

Steven Pressfield, Author of *The War of Art* poses the question, "are we so obsessed with healing and wellness because we are so afraid to die early without having actually lived yet?" He references the "healing" subculture:
"The concept in all these environments seems to be that one needs to complete his healing before he is ready to do his work. This way of thinking.... is a form of Resistance. What are we trying to heal, anyway? The athlete knows the day will never come when he wakes up pain-free. He has to play hurt." [11]

We have to play hurt sometimes. We have to live *before* we feel better.

* * *

Chinese Medicine practitioner Lonny Jarrett will try to assess the degree to which patients are focused on their reasons and inability to heal. From his book *Deepening Perspectives* he says,

> *"Often I ask a patient who is expressing pain and hopelessness regarding the complexity of a trauma if they are "aware of any dimension of their experience where there is no problem"* [4]

He explains that there is a more positive prognosis the quicker they can shift attention to that part of the self already whole.

> *"Although healing the body takes time, the most substantial part of psycho-emotional healing takes none because the sense of having a problem is based on the misappropriation of attention and requires merely a shift of focus from one dimension of experience to another...*
>
> *...Frequently, the so-called blocks to integrity that we imagine within and without are merely projections of the ego's addiction to a sense of "problem" as a way of buying time. For ego has had its connection to wholeness, to origin, severed at the root, and it is not a condition that it can imagine."* [12]

Many of us have lost our connection to the state of being healed altogether. Over time, the reasons we have for not being ready yet become temporarily self-replenishing. We may resolve one set of symptoms, but then we uncover a traumatic event from childhood during therapy. We may come to terms with something that once triggered us, but we are still sick from a moldy house we used to live in.

Whatever it is, there is always another reason. They never end.

They never will in fact, as dismal as it sounds. But the never-ending justification for continued healing serves as a very effective protection for the terrifying reality of actually being healed. Being healed would mean that we don't have reasons anymore. We don't have anything in the way of us pursuing success, and a life that really matters to us. We don't have an obvious roadblock to explain away our lack of certain life accomplishments we believe we should have achieved, if we were well. The worst part of it all is that to be healed is to be stripped of our identity of one who is healing. Of someone on a valiant struggle of fighting demons of the mind and body. We lose the merit that comes with the hardship of an illness or a heart-breaking past (the story). We lose our edge. It is painfully revealed that we don't know who we are if we are not healing. Being healed leaves us bare. So we cling to our reasons like armor, a uniform. They protect us and affirm our identity. Our reasons give us more time. Indefinitely.

This works really well for a while, but eventually we all get a knock at the door. Except this door is the one inside of us, from the dark basement. And the knocking is our own Soul.

.

"*The time it takes for us to live up to our deeper and higher realizations is just as long as we want it to.*"

-Lonny Jarrett [13]

5

The Call: The Unconscious

The idea of the soul is further intimidating because it asks something of us; that is it summons ego consciousness to an accounting. The soul asks us to a larger frame of reference, to an eternal perspective amid our time-bound egos and their reductive, fear-driven agendas. Such a presence reminds us that we are never alone when alone, that there is another that provides continuity to our fractured days, organic unity to our broken selves, and transcendence to our fallen condition. The soul is intuited in childhood, pushed aside by adaptive choices of consciousness, and recovered in adulthood only when we are willing to open to it.
-James Hollis [14]

Writing about the unconscious is not new and I am not an expert on the matter. I will leave the deeper discussion for the Jungian scholars such as James Hollis, J. Gary Sparks, Robert A. Johnson, and Carl Jung himself, among others that have already been mentioned. I recommend reading their published works if you're interested, or better yet, engage in Jungian analysis yourself.

But we can talk about the ways the unconscious calls to us in our lives even without a deep psychological or psychoanalytic understanding of it. Of course it is tricky because we are attempting to use our conscious minds to consider the very part of us that is not conscious, and to draw some sort of bridge between the two.

Jung reminds us that "whatever we have to say about the unconscious is what the conscious mind says about it. Always the unconscious psyche, which is entirely of an unknown nature, is expressed by consciousness and in terms of consciousness, and that is the only thing we can do. We cannot go beyond that, and we should always keep it in mind as an ultimate critique of our judgment". [15]

But if we contemplate that for a moment, it is clearly important work. There is such a large proportion of ourselves that we pay hardly any attention to while most of our energy is aimed at the part that keeps us alive day to day. We need to survive each day, but we are also here to live something deeper. After all, we don't simply die after we procreate and raise our young to independence. What is being asked of us is something much greater than that. However, anything greater, or larger, than whatever we currently are inherently involves the unknown. It requires moving into space that we don't inhabit yet. It is likely going to involve a steep learning curve, and risk, and loss. Failure is almost certain.

If the need for more healing is a belief, we have to be able to change our minds in order to heal.

* * *

Just as each small stroke on a canvas can't step aside to see the whole painting, we're unable to take in the great whole of relationships and counterbalance that surrounds us in all directions.
Our inability to comprehend the inner workings of the universe may actually bring us more in tune with its infinitude. The magic is not in the analyzing or the understanding. The magic lives in the wonder of what we do not know.

-Rick Rubin [16]

This *will* involve some level of pain to the part of us that finds comfort in what is known and familiar, and in what we can control. While being unwell is clearly not pleasant, it is a familiar way of being. If we are still in the process of healing, then we cannot be expected to pursue what our healed selves would be capable of. If we examine the part of us that isn't consumed with daily survival and distraction, that is really where our greater perspective lies, the knowing of the Soul. If we maintain attention on only our conscious, partial self, we ignore deeply meaningful aspects of our existence. Eventually, if we never go into the unconscious, the Soul will find a way to call to us in our conscious lives.

"Consciousness is always only a part of the psyche, and therefore never capable of psychic wholeness: for that the indefinite extension of the unconscious is needed. But the unconscious can neither be caught with clever formulas nor exorcised by means of scientific dogmas, for something of destiny clings to it - indeed, it is sometimes destiny itself".
-Carl Jung [17]

James Hollis is explaining that we won't be able to think ourselves whole, as our thinking function is inherently partial. We won't be able to use known, familiar tools to understand the unconscious content that our Soul wants us to integrate. And ultimately, we won't have a choice in whether we meet the Soul or not.

In his book Inner Work, Robert A. Johnson says, *"Most of the time we are not very aware of what we do, or why we do it. Our behavior is generated by the values that we serve, by those inner beliefs and attitudes that we have discussed. One of the best ways to discover what you really believe, what value you are really serving, is to watch your own behavior..."*

We may be convinced that we value being healed and really living our life while we have the chance. But does our behavior confirm this? Johnson explains that we may think we believe in certain values, but when we look and see what it is that we actually do, it *".reveals a completely different set of beliefs controlling you, a different value system than the one you profess".*
[18]

It is like there are parts of us at work that we don't even know about, whilst believing that we have the whole story. We can only fool ourselves for so long.

The irony of getting a call from the Soul is that often it appears in the form of physical symptoms, or psycho-emotional symptoms. Ironically, we could choose to use the symptoms as further *reasons*. Simply add them into our proof of illness. But there is something nagging about them that is just different. There is an unease. A tension. A seeping anxiety that begins to permeate our once peaceful moments. We may set aside time to rest because we are so fatigued by our ailments. We convince ourselves that we need to check out from the world. It's all too much. We are unwell after all. But often when we have gotten comfortable, canceled our plans, tucked into a show or social media, there is something beneath the relief that we initially felt when justifying our needs for self-care and rest.

Under the comfort something is a little bit off. But it's easy to ignore for a while. We are doing *the work*. We have assured ourselves from all angles that it is all justified. But there is still something unsettled living just beyond our most conscious grasp. We can almost blink it away and get back to what we are doing.

But our Soul knows that we are here for more than just aiming for ground zero. Healing implies that we are in the negative. We are always catching up to being just the minimum. Our Soul has much bigger plans than that. It can be very patient for some time while we act out our various mechanisms keeping us safe in our known, comfortable position. But after a while, as our time here diminishes, things become more urgent. The Soul has increasingly less opportunity to carry out its purpose as our body ages and our cognitive faculties decline. The Soul knows it is falling short on carrying out its part of the evolution of the whole. So it comes knocking.

We can ignore the knocking for a while, a very long time even. We can placate and soothe and distract for years. We can collect all the reasons for not being ready to listen. Somewhere inside of us knows that if we take the call, something will have to change. In fear, we ignore it, with compelling justification. But someday the knocking will grow louder and eventually it will knock down the door altogether. We will find ourselves in a medical emergency, or financially destitute. We will be in the midst of a divorce or losing our home. Something to shake us finally into paying attention. It is not uncommon for people to radically change their entire lives upon receiving a cancer diagnosis. Suddenly they are pursuing their dream vocation, spending quality time with loved ones, and no longer living through semi-convincingly meaningful distractions that keep them comfortable and stagnant. They simply answer the call.

Why does it take some of us such dire circumstances to finally hear what the Soul is asking of us? Because, while we ignore it, we already know that it will require great change. It will require us to relinquish the need for more time, for further healing, for being a victim of others. Being healed is not about the disappearance of symptoms, or erasure of the past. It is simply being done with needing more time before we do what we are really here to do. It is giving up an imagined, prerequisite state of happiness and thriving in order to take on a life that really matters to us. It is doing it now, anyway. It is answering the call *while* we have symptoms, in the midst of anxiety. It is willingly engaging in the content of our unconscious, without filter or safety assurance. It isn't successfully easing our nerves, alleviating anxiety, or eradicating fear. It isn't sinking deep into our fatigue and pulling the soft blanket of avoidance over our heads. It is walking towards the Soul's ringing call, crawling if needed, in pain even, and picking it up, and listening.

.

The enigma at the heart of quantum reality can be summed up in a simple motto: what we see when we look at the world seems to be fundamentally different from what actually is.
    -Sean Carroll, theoretical physicist[19]

6

The Responsibility: The Duty

Despite how greatly some people may suffer, the prospect of being free from their suffering seems to scare them even more than the true possibility that suffering may never abate. In part, this is because the mind is more comfortable with what is known. In the face of the unknown, it habitually and irrationally chooses to cling to the status quo, even if that means suffering.

-Lonny Jarrett [20]

In one of Franz Kafka's letters he reflects on his terrible fear of dying, because he has not yet lived. The famous quote is :"I could live and I do not live". [21]

Imagine you found a suspicious lump on our body. You may spend some time ignoring it, hoping it will go away on its own. But say after some time you come across it again and it's larger than before. You might reassure yourself that it was always that way. But then it becomes painful. It starts restricting movement. Other symptoms develop. You are more tired, not sleeping. Eventually you become so worried that you make an appointment with the doctor. They run some tests, do a scan, and take a biopsy. They tell you they will give you a call with the results. You go home and try not to think about it but you are terrified of what the results will be. Yes, you are scared of dying, but also scared of what measures you will have to take in order to not die. What drastic changes will be in order. You wait and wait and then the phone finally rings. They call you in to discuss. When you get to your appointment the doctor hands you a report with their findings. He tells you that you indeed have a form of cancer, but that there are options. If you are diligent, you will be okay. If not, you will likely die, and suffer terribly in the meantime. So you get to work. Your life depends on it after all.

——

Now say that instead of discussing your options and the changes you would be making, you left the office, drove home, and threw the report in the trash. Then you went about your life as normal. It sounds absurd because it is! In reality, you would likely reconsider your job, how much money you make and how much stress it puts on your body. You'd consider how much time you spend working, then how much is spent on distractions of mediocre entertainment and comfort. You'd reevaluate your efforts at caring for your body. Your diet, your exercise, your quality of sleep and the health of your environment would suddenly become of great interest. You'd make genuine efforts to reduce the negatives in your life, easily slashing many of them in a moment. You'd prioritize spending time with your loved ones far more than other activities. You might finally do that thing you've always wanted to do. You'd make a change. You'd use energy and put in effort. You'd find yourself with more energy for more effort, for more work. It would light a fire under you.

It is the same with heeding the call from the Soul. It isn't enough just to answer the call and write the message down on a notepad and forget about it. It's up to you now to do something about it. It sounds harsh, and I suppose it is. But not for nothing. *It is for everything.* It is not even just for our own lives and pursuing what is truly meaningful to us. It goes beyond that because we are a small, but critical part of everything and everyone. How could it be any other way? We exist, and everything else exists. What we do next will regress or evolve the whole. Even if we simply stay as we are, it is not mere stagnation. Time moves forward, relentlessly. Entropy increases. If we stay put, we begin to draw tension on the inevitable movement that is required of all life. Existence keeps moving and we must drive our heels in to avoid going forth. Over time, this is extremely fatiguing. We mistake the fatigue as a need for rest, but it is really a need to move! It is a need to change, to grow.

As Rick Rubin says,

> *"It's helpful to work as if the project you're engaged in is bigger than you".* [22]

While his background is in art and music production, and his book on a whole is about the creative act of being, this quote is from his chapter on Self-awareness. We can think of our life as one big creative act. If we engage in our life as though it is bigger than us, how will that be different than thinking our life is as small as a single person in a moment of time?

When we understand that our unwillingness to evolve pulls back on the whole of everyone and everything, then we can really understand that it is not only in our best interests to heal, but it is our responsibility to transform what we think is our personal pain, and understand that it is the pain of the whole. A small, minuscule portion yes, but a part in a whole. In this context, responsibility grows into duty.

There is a great purpose then, in being healed.

* * *

I invite you now to read a more lengthy quote from one of Jung's famous lectures on Analytical Psychology in 1935. To grasp the full meaning, it's helpful to introduce (or recap for many of you) the idea of the collective unconscious. Through Jung's travels visiting foreign countries, 'primitive' cultures, and inpatients in psychiatric wards around the world, he found that many people dreamed of great symbols and mythologies that they would never have come across in their personal lives. With countless observations such as these, years of clinical work with his own patients, and education in ancient cultures such as those of India and China, he came to the understanding of the collective unconscious and how it appeared in dreams. Those images that patients had a personal association with were part of their personal unconscious, while the greater symbols were part of the unconscious of all of us. Hence, the collective unconscious. These images he called archetypes. This brief explanation should aid in the effect of the following piece of the lecture:

> *"[In relation to a particular dream of a former patient] This dream contains an archetypal image, and that is always an indication that the psychological situation of the dreamer extends beyond the mere personal layer of the unconscious. **His problem is no more***

entirely a personal affair, but something which touches upon the problems of mankind in general....

*....Modern therapy is not much aware of this, but in ancient medicine it was well known that **the raising of the personal disease to a higher and more impersonal level had a curative effect....***

*....If the archetypal situation underlying the illness can be expressed in the right way the patient is cured. If no adequate expression is found, the individual is thrown back upon himself, into the isolation of being ill; he is alone and has no connection with the world. **But if he is shown that his particular ailment is not his ailment only, but a general ailment** - even a god's ailment - he is in the company of men and gods, and **this knowledge produces a healing effect.... The individual is lifted out of his miserable loneliness and represented as undergoing a heroic meaningful fate which is ultimately good for the whole world,** like the suffering and death of a god.... And so it is quite likely that an impressive and adequate symbol can mobilize the forces of the unconscious to such an extent that even the nervous system becomes affected and the body begins to react in a normal way again....*

*....In the case of psychological suffering, which always isolates the individual from the herd of so-called normal people, it is also of the greatest importance to understand that the conflict is not a personal failure only, but at the same time a suffering common to all and a problem with which the whole epoch is burdened. **This general point of view lifts the individual out of himself and connects him with humanity.***"

-Carl Jung [23]

* * *

All the while that we are still healing, we are creating tension on the whole of evolution. Or to put it differently, we are severing our greater connection to the world and missing our opportunity to heal a part of everyone's suffering. Again, being healed does not require us to be symptom free, for the diagnosis to vanish, and our past traumas to rewrite themselves. But being healed is how we will relate to those aspects of reality. What conclusions we draw from them, and the limitations we have inferred. Is it possible to do what is needed, even *while* we are in pain? When we exercise, we do not rest afterward in order to lose progress. We do it to *recover* enough so that we can go further the next time. If we rest too much, we lose our strength and we become weak. Many injuries in fact are better healed not from ceasing activity, but from modifying it in such a way that we can keep going, maintaining healthy blood flow and circulation. Strengthening our bodies is our responsibility to ourselves in order to carry out what we need to in life in order to survive and succeed. Evolving our own selves and carrying out what is asked of us by our whole self is our responsibility to our existence. It is our duty to everyone.

———

One of the hardest parts about responsibility is that we are not only responsible for our own success. We are responsible for our entire life as adults. This means that no matter what has happened to us, or what we have been forced to endure, we are still responsible. Until we take one thousand percent accountability for our lives, we cannot enact the necessary changes to live out a life of meaning. If we indulge in any fraction of blame on others, on illness, on unfairness, on struggle, on the *past*, then we are removing our own responsibility in taking the call, in making the change, in growing up. It is *true* that we have been wronged. It is *true* that we have suffered an accident, an illness, a trauma. It is so hard and painful and real. And it is also true that it's our responsibility. No matter how terrible things done to us were.

Who is responsible if not us?

Someone can apologize or try to make amends. Or they may not. They may be dead. They may not intend to apologize. There are so many variables involved that do not change how much we are still responsible for our own lives. We may have been put in debt by wrongdoings of others. They may pay us back, they may not. The time lost will never be recovered regardless. We are responsible regardless. We can wait around for our entire lives for others to make it right. For us to heal.

The truth is that even if every wrong doing was somehow accounted for, we would still be making excuses for why we cannot pursue a life of meaning, unless we take responsibility for ourselves. If we let everyone else take responsibility, we can longer evolve. We are like infants again, totally dependent on others just for mere survival.

In order to take responsibility, we have to give up blame entirely. No matter how justified. No matter how real, how wrong. The blame only serves to add to our list of reasons. To add to the ever increasing time that is needed for healing. To avoid doing what really matters to us.

* * *

Consider this thought:

> *"Ethics is a principle of unity and consistency. People who behave ethically are those who make an honest effort to conform their behavior to their values. If one's conduct is grossly at odds with one's essential character, it always reflects a fragmentation of the personality. As Jung said, 'A shirking of ethical responsibility...deprives him of his wholeness and imposes a painful fragmentariness on his life"*

-Robert A. Johnson [24]

It is simply not enough to *understand* our duty to the whole. If we do not act in it with 100% integrity, it means very little. In fact, to know it and to *not act* on it is an even worse affront to our Soul.

> *"Consider your craft as an energy alive in you. It's just as much a part of the cycle of evolution as other living things are. It wants to grow. It wants to flower. To hone your craft is to honor creation. It doesn't matter if you become the best in your field. By practicing to improve, you are fulfilling your ultimate purpose on this planet."*

-Rick Rubin [25]

Your life's purpose *is* your craft. Living your life as your own creative act and fulfilling your own purpose, may evolve only a tiny thread, but the thread is a part of the whole. So we do our part in evolving the whole by doing our very best with our own life. If we are always healing, we will never contribute to the whole of evolution. And we will be tormented at a soul level as a result.

Once we answer the call and confront what matters to us, what is meaningful, we then have the responsibility to live it out. Fully. Relentlessly. That is the risk of being healed. Once we are healed, we have no more reasons. We are left totally bare. If we fail, we simply wear the pain of failure. We are forced to face the job we must leave, or the relationship that is entirely wrong for us. Or perhaps no concrete change is needed at all but rather our entire relationship with life and the conclusions we've drawn about the world. Many of our beliefs we were not have been even aware of, that were keeping us safely stuck for our whole lives.

The truth is that the responsibility was already ours. The duty was already there. Always healing and never healed is just our way of ignoring that. But taking on our duty is the best thing we could ever do. Even with our symptoms in tow. Our duty will never be impossible for us. It exists just *for us*. It exists *because* we exist. No illness or trauma will be too much to stand in the way of it. In fact, those events, terrible as they are, will likely provide us with insight and experience we need in order to carry out something much bigger than the healing process itself. So we must heed the call, release all blame, take responsibility, and finish healing once and for all. The duty is ours.

.

43

Those who have the privilege to know have the duty to act
-Albert Einstein

7

The Challenge: The Training

We have to give up our reasons, our time. We have to be responsible for all of the horrible experiences that have happened in our lives. We have to grow up and fulfill our duty to the entirety of existence. It's big. It's a lot. It's also a little bit abstract at this point. What does it really *mean* to fulfill our duty? How do we know what we're supposed to do here? And say we figure out that part, how do we actually do it? We may be weak and tired or totally broken by life at this point (see:reasons chapter) so how on earth are we supposed to just flip a switch and suddenly take on the tasks of the world at large? That sounds hard.

I want to bring some kindness and softness into it, and also be real. No doubt, it *is* hard. It will be hard. But the hard that comes from truly growing up, relinquishing blame, letting our fear and anxiety move us rather than depress us- that is entirely different than the hard we experience being unwell, justifying our illness and incapacity, and ultimately missing out on a life that really means something to us. The latter hard will ruin us to our Soul level. That is harsher than any challenge we will face in the pursuit of a meaningful life.

Many people who are caught in the still healing process will use tools that are arguably beneficial, but that only serve to perpetuate their status quo. Meditation is one such tool and is no doubt useful for, as Lonny Jarrett says, *"empowering a relative degree of ease and objectivity in the face of the unknown".* However, *"the only practical manifestation of meditation is our quality of motivation evidenced in the choices that we make when not meditating."* [26]

Our 'training' becomes another trap if it only serves to put us at more ease in our perpetual healing process, rather than facing the unknown in the choice to be healed.

My wish is that no one gets to the end and wants to bargain with life to let them do it over, and *really* live their life this time. I want us to be comfortable and safe and at ease, but not if it costs us everything that we're really here to do. In the end we die anyway of course, but why are we here in the first place? No one can say definitively what the meaning of life is, but anyone who pays attention for even a moment *knows* when they're not doing it. We know, somewhere in us, when we are wasting our own time and copping out. We know that under a lot of the comfort we choose that we are missing the bigger life. We rationalize that we will choose it later, once we are more rested or better prepared. Once we are no longer sick or damaged. *Then* we will live the life we are here to live.

So by all means, take the time that is *really* necessary to address urgent needs of recovery and survival or life crises and emergencies. Get adequate sleep, dietary nourishment, and physical movement. Do your daily practices to reduce chronic stress and regulate your nervous system. But beyond those necessary activities that will give us strength and resilience, do not waste a moment more. It's alarming to even acknowledge that sentence if we're in the habit of needing more time. But truly, in real honesty with ourselves, we wouldn't waste a moment more.

* * *

If your mind would appreciate some practical tools to increase its likelihood of success in this endeavor, there is a kind of training that we can engage in. As a forewarning, the training is hard, by design. In fact, the point of the training is to help us embrace the challenge that is inherent in the shift, and the consistent effort that comes *afterwards*, forever. The good news is that just like overall stress from both positive and negative activities is difficult for our systems to differentiate, so too can challenge and hardship in one area create resilience for our whole person. For instance, we can access mental resilience by using challenges of the physical body. *Challenge* itself will be highly subjective depending on the level of suffering that someone has already endured or avoided and the psychological resilience that has been lost or gained in the process. Physical activity may be a release for some and a punishment for others. Don't pick a challenge practice that is not really a challenge for you, or it won't work. If you do, you know that it's another way of buying more time, ticking a box to prove you're working towards something while you're actually looping back around. I'll list some ideas below and it will be up to you to determine if they will push you into discomfort or not. As a grown up, you can determine if any option is detrimental to your health and choose something else. But be honest and be wary of reasons that are not genuine.

Another note of caution: the training is not something you need to do *before* pursuing whatever it is that gives you anxiety and is of extreme importance. You don't have to do it at all. But you can do it alongside what really matters to help prepare for the inevitable twist and turns along the way.

* * *

The suggestions:

1. Strenuous activity first thing in the morning

If you are usually slow to start and feel sluggish and unmotivated in the mornings, this is a good option. 'Strenuous' will be scale-able depending on your experience, and will have to be ramped up as you adapt and improve your conditioning. If you're more comfortable with cardio, choose resistance training. If you love lifting weights, go out for a run or bike ride.

2. Waking up early

Following on from the first idea, if you tend to stay in bed avoiding the day, a good challenge training is to force yourself to get up early. This likely involves setting an alarm. A good rule is to have no snooze option. Don't even contemplate whether or not you'll get up. Don't look for motivation. If you're motivated to get up, it's no longer your challenge training. See what it's like to watch your mind go over all its *reasons* to stay in bed, why it needs more rest, more time….then get up anyway.

3. Carrying heavy things

This is a simple and easily scale-able activity that can really test our willingness to train into struggle and it's resulting resilience. If you have a heavy medicine ball or weight, you can carry it around your backyard or home. Better yet, get a sturdy backpack and put some weights into it and head out for a walk. You'll learn quickly how much heavier the weight becomes over a short distance. Don't get hurt obviously, but struggle. Do it a couple of times a week and see if you can walk further or add more weight over time to maintain the challenge. If it gets easy, find some stairs!

4. Heat and/or Cold

Temperature alteration is an easy way to put ourselves quickly out of ease, despite its potential health benefits. Do your due diligence to ensure you are in such condition to sustain high or low temperatures. If doing heat, a traditional dry sauna is a great option for training. Cold can be done simply with a shower, a bath, or cold weather with minimal clothing. You can personalize the practice easily by staying put in the heat or cold until you start hearing the reasons to get out. In this way you can train your resilience by staying longer, experiencing the discomfort.

5. Write

If you love strenuous physical activity and you regularly exercise already, it may be more useful for you to choose something that challenges your mental attention, your patience, your creativity. Choose a time every single day to sit down and write. Write at least 1,000 words, every day. This may seem easy and silly to many of you, but to some it will be excruciating. Again, you may notice that your mind comes up with many reasons why it's a waste of time, why you have more important things to do. That's perfect. Having reasons not to, and doing it anyway, you're training yourself for the challenge. You will get better at hearing the reasons, knowing already that they are empty, and moving forward.

6. Make a phone call - strike up conversation

For the more introvertedly inclined, it's easy to hide in any of the options above, sitting out discomfort valiantly in the very comfort of your own isolation. If you often shy away from connecting with others, if it makes you sweaty and sick feeling when you get an unexpected phone call, this might be a great option for you. Instead of sending a text or email to your family member, pick up the phone and call them. Practice striking up conversations when you are out in public. Do it everyday. It doesn't have to be long or drawn out. Likely, the most uncomfortable part will be anticipating that you're going to do this, and the first moments that you actually attempt it. Having a chat with someone is often really beneficial and makes us feel a greater sense of belonging. It's okay if you come out of it with a feeling of connectedness, which is wonderful. Keep practicing the part that is hard, and you will still reap the benefits of resilience.

7. Be alone and do nothing

Again, for some, being in solitude may be your comfort zone. If that's the case, choose something else. But if you tend to use alone time to distract yourself by watching shows on your laptop, scrolling on your phone, or even reading a book, this may be an appropriate training option. Schedule out time each day to do nothing. It may sound relaxing but many people will quickly begin to squirm. In fact, sometimes this is the hardest task of all because there is nothing to drown out the reasons voice that is persuading us to stop. This can be very powerful and may take some practice. You may find yourself giving up after five minutes and checking your phone, answering emails, or reading the back labels on the food in your pantry. Try to push it to six minutes next time.

You may notice how these activities, while challenging, are actually quite beneficial for us. Most of them, to some extent, will create resistance in us. They require a level of suffering and pain. While the point here is about experiencing the suffering itself, it is not inconsequential that we also derive benefit as a result. In fact, in some cases, the benefit is a direct response to the suffering, such as micro damage to our muscles in exercise that leads to stronger muscles as they repair. So there are layers to resilience that begin to emerge. What is it really? Is it becoming increasingly strong in body and mind, more able to endure struggle as a result of greater fitness? Yes. Is it the practice of enduring struggle to the extent that we are better able to endure the struggle we face in the future? Yes. It is all the same. Training resilience makes us better people, and it also makes us those kinds of people that can continue to do what's best, even if we face hardship in the process.

* * *

There are two things I want to make note of here. The first is that whatever it is we are healing from will be accompanied by any number of very real limitations to our physical and mental abilities. We talked about this earlier but the state of being 'healed' in this context is about our relationship to the world and our conclusions about ourselves in it. It doesn't mean that there won't be symptoms, limitations, pain etc. It just means that we do not view those as impediments to living a life of meaning and starting *right now* in our pursuit of what matters most to us. The real medicine is what helps us address those issues as we move forward, rather than keeping us in an ongoing healing process as a prerequisite to our *real* lives.

The second item is that there is an important difference between challenge training and simply sticking with a bad situation in life. We cannot choose, for instance, an abusive relationship and call that our training. Often these are the situations that we are unable to get out of when we are in the 'always healing' mindset because we do not believe we have the strength and ability to leave or be on our own, or that we lack certain resources. If the circumstance is such that it is outside of our control to exit for the time being, then we can apply the training mindset in order to endure it until we are able to make a change. These are the times where prior training really comes in handy. As our life changes, so too will the training and its application.

* * *

As one personal example, when I was a couple of years into a complex and bewildering tick-borne bacterial illness, I happened upon a Brazilian Jiu Jitsu class at a festival a few hours from where I lived in Melbourne, Australia. I loved it so much that I signed up for classes as soon as I got home. I didn't realize how much harder the actual training would be and I was really worried that my body wouldn't be up for it, considering what I perceived of my physical state. I had already made the commitment and signed a membership contract so I decided to just go and do my best. It was the perfect type of training I knew I needed to get out of the depressive hole I had been in about my health. It was hard and had a steep learning curve so I was challenged physically and intellectually, and I was brand new in a room of what seemed like much more experienced students. I went to every Jiu Jitsu class on the schedule and even added in kickboxing classes 4 nights a week. I quickly realized that not only could my body handle much more than I anticipated, but I actually had no resistance to the training at all. In fact, I was more concerned with other life commitments *preventing me* from getting there. It quickly lost its challenge factor as a viable resilience training, despite the difficulty. It just didn't create anxiety, fear, fatigue, or a reach for any reasons. That was until I attended my first wrestling class.

Friday nights were for wrestling. The focus was on takedowns, going from the feet to the floor. I remember during the warm-ups one of the other students said, 'first wrestling class? Welcome to hell', and then laughed. I laughed too, sort of. I picked up the technique fairly well, but it was new and different to jiu jitsu. Then the drills began and it was much more physically taxing getting taken to the floor, getting up, and taking down my partner. Then we began the live sparring portion. I couldn't remember any of the techniques I had learned. I got slammed into the ground over and over. All of my alarm signals went off and I had to keep getting up and starting again. When class finally ended I was so relieved I wanted to burst into tears. I did *not* like wrestling and I did not want to do that class ever again. I changed my shirt for Jiu Jitsu scheduled next, welcoming the comfortable familiarity.

On the way home I thought about the class. I was in the midst of shifting my attention from my identity as a sick person who couldn't do this or that, to someone who could try anything and experience the difficulty of it. I realized, with horror, that wrestling was the perfect way to actually do this. It didn't work for Jiu Jitsu, I loved it too much. It came with ease. So I committed to going to wrestling every Friday night. By Wednesday I would feel sick to my stomach about it and come 6pm Friday I was in sheer terror. And I did this every week without fail for years.

Overtime I got better at wrestling. I realized how much heavier most of my male training partners were and how many of them were much newer than I realized, and hadn't learned proper technique or control over themselves either. As we all improved, the training became more enjoyable, even though still physically demanding. I no longer felt as nervous before class. In fact, Jiu Jitsu started developing a greater challenge aspect. I had a few concussions and other injuries over the years. Everyone was improving and my initial affinity for the sport mattered little anymore now that we had all developed technique. The heavier opponents now also had skill. In addition, much of the classes involved technique I had already learned, but now needed to refine. It wasn't all novel and exciting everyday. It was still incredibly fun, but there was a grind now. I kept doing wrestling, kickboxing, all of the classes, but the resilience training shifted around and at times I had to look for it elsewhere in life.

* * *

Being an artist
means to be continually asking,
"How can it be better?"
whatever it is.
It may be your art,
And it may be your life.
-Rick Rubin [27]

It's not about asking what else can I heal, in order to remain in the healing process, as a way of "bettering myself". It means being healed,

53

so we can truly ask this question, and go forth to pursue the better life, without needing more healing first.

Humans are incredibly adaptive beings and over time, we will likely become more comfortable with our chosen challenges. This is of course positive as we become stronger, faster, more open to connection, more creative, more at ease in our own company. It just means we may need to change our training over time, either to something new or to a greater scale, or add a variable. Eventually though, you may find that the training starts to merge with the rest of your life. Difficult tasks don't create as much resistance, or the resistance doesn't deter you as much. Impending circumstances may still create doom, but it doesn't impede your efforts at engaging in them in earnest.

Soon you are just someone who can do hard things.

You are no longer focusing on the part of yourself that says this is hard and therefore I can't do it, or the part that reaches for the list of reasons each time you are faced with the possibility of challenge and discomfort. And that is what the training is for. Not for endless, increasingly harder training, but for your life. You are not really training what you can do, you are genuinely training who you are and how you approach, and respond, to life's tasks.

Living in discovery is at all times preferable to living through assumptions.
-Rick Rubin [28]

8

The Decision: The Shift

*The Soul's sincerity of longing for rectification for the sake of
greater integrity is complimented by heaven's grace. Regardless of
how neglected the soul is, it remains capable of responding the
instant the we turn attention to it. This is a kindness that can
bring us to our knees when we first realize how we have been
living as compared with what we've intuited the possibility of life
is in that deepest and best part of ourselves. When we step an inch
toward the soul it springs to life, taking 100 steps toward us, no
matter how neglected it has been. In one moment it is reborn,
flooding awareness like an ocean.*
-Lonny Jarrett [29]

The truth is, the shift can be done in an instant. No training, no time. The human element means that we often do not do what can be done, usually against our own conscious wishes, (why engaging with the unconscious content is key). But the shift is available now. As Lonny Jarrett explains, our attention is on our partial self, the part that has a problem, that is wounded, that needs more time. It's not that this part is not expressing a true belief, it's that it's only a partial truth. When we shift or expand our attention to contain our entire self, the whole truth, then we see that we are already healed, we're already whole, and we've never been anything but whole. And then we must accept this 100%. Jarrett continues the quote above though, pointing out,

> *"....That 'turning point' is the moment that is most crucial and recovery is most tender. For once we awaken to soul, if we turn our back on it we engender cynicism, a bitterness that slowly poisons the heart."*
> -Lonny Jarrett [30]

Once we get it, once we know better, we cannot rewind back into denial. We cannot pretend that we didn't take the call and run back to our reasons and time. We may feign ignorance but it won't be the same as before, when we really believed it. We may even try to convince ourselves that the healing really is our path, and our true calling.

In The War of Art, Steven Pressfield writes,

> *"Remember, the part of us that we imagine needs healing is not the part we create from; that part is far deeper and stronger. The part we create from can't be touched by anything our parents did, or society did. That part is unsullied, uncorrupted; soundproof, waterproof, and bulletproof."* [31]

Our whole self that contains our Soul cannot be anything *but* whole. Parts of us can experience absolute brutality, betrayal, loss and illness, and it is still only a part of a whole self that is always whole. Parts of the whole experience pain and destruction, and are still part of the whole. The healing is not about directing our attention to the broken parts and endlessly rearranging them to try to fit it all back together. The healing is shifting the attention, zooming out to acknowledge all of it, including the broken parts over there at the edge. This is how we shift from healing towards evolution.

* * *

One of the most important statements is reinforced several times in Lonny Jarrett's book *Deepening Perspectives*, written for practitioners who work with those making this shift.

> *"To the degree that we are un-enlightened, the past is the most significant influence in determining who we are in any given moment. To the degree that we are awakened to, and taken responsibility for the self, the future is the most significant input into who we are....*
> *....Awakening entails a shift of attention from overcoming the past to the creation of a better, more wholesome future"*
> -Lonny Jarrett [32]

The shift itself is only a momentary redirection of attention in the end. Ultimately, it takes no time, and no effort even. In fact, it takes more effort to maintain a fixed attention on a single, partial aspect. This aspect is the part of us that believes we need to expend all of our resources healing. Thinking about healing, talking about healing, spending money and time and energy on healing. We become so identified with being in a healing process and being someone who is damaged, that it is very unsettling to relinquish this persona. It won't happen on its own for this reason, so it's up to us to make the decision. And we can't make the decision and then pay attention to all the little conditions that start filtering in about how we *will* do it but just *after* we finish this next course on such and such condition, or once we go to another ceremony, or stick with this special diet a little longer. Making the decision does not negate the need to care for ourselves and continue to improve our health. Making the decision means we give up the need for more time, we give up the right to blame others for where we are in life, we take full responsibility for our life and all of our decisions, and we complete the healing process. We make the shift from the partial self to the whole self, the healing self to the already healed self, and we move forward from there. Medicine can then be used to clean up the remaining symptoms, to further improve our state of being, and to address the collateral damage that comes with pursuing a life that really means something to us.

* * *

If we do continue to engage with medicine to assist us in this way, we must be cautious about who we choose to work with. If the practitioner has not made the shift, their approach to their medicine will focus only on the aspect of you that is wounded, and will only serve to perpetuate the need for healing even further.

"From an integral perspective, it is assumed that the practitioner's own integrity in this regard is the foundation of efficacy in medicine. Practically, that means the practitioner has renounced needing any more time in life for their own healing because they are fundamentally identified with the dimension of self that is already whole. Their attention is always relatively more focused on manifesting future potential than on overcoming past wounds or the pursuit of pleasure as an escape from an uncomfortable past or present"
  -Lonny Jarrett [33]

Choose your medicine wisely and always keep in mind that ultimately we are the ones responsible for our life, even if we seek assistance for certain attributes. Being responsible means it's all on us now, and there is no better way for it to be. Not blaming others means that it's completely within our volition to create a life that has purpose *to us*. Once we make the shift it doesn't suddenly become easy. We don't suddenly become free of pain. Life may require *more effort* in fact as we now have the opportunity to fulfill our unique task here as part of an even greater whole. That's what the training is for. There is nothing left to linger on at this point. We don't even need to revisit a bookmarked page, or save an idea to work on later. Make the decision, and make the shift. No longer healing, already healed.

.

From a spiritual perspective, the single most fundamentally important choice that any human makes is on what dimension of experience they place attention.

-Lonny Jarrett [34]

Bibliography

Carroll, Sean. *Something Deeply Hidden: Quantum Worlds and the Emergence of Spacetime.* New York: Penguin Publishing Group, 2019.

Hollis, James. *Finding Meaning in the Second Half of Life: How to Finally, Really Grow Up.* 1st ed. New York: Gotham Books, 2006.

Jarrett, Lonny. *Deepening Perspectives on Chinese Medicine.* 1st ed. Massachusetts: Spirit Path press, 2021.

Johnson, Robert A. *Inner Work: Using Dreams and Active Imagination for Personal Growth.* 1st ed. New York: Harper One, 1989.

Jung, Carl. *Analytical Psychology: Its Theory and Practice.* 2nd ed. London: Taylor and Francis Group, 2014.

Pressfield, Steven. *The War of Art: Break Through Your Blocks and Win Your Inner Creative Battles.* 1st ed. New York: Rugged Land LLC, 2002;

Rubin, Rick. *The Creative Act: A Way of Being.* New York: Penguin Publishing Group, 2023.

Recommended Reading

Bisset, Alison. *Choose Anxiety: Actions and Considerations for Anxious People who want to Evolve and why Alleviating Anxiety isn't the way.* A. Bisset, 2022.

Frenkel, Edward. *Love and Math: The Heart of Hidden Reality.* New York: Basic Books, 2014.

Hollis, James. *Living an Examined Life: Wisdom For the Second Half of the Journey.* Colorado: Sounds True, 2018.

Jarrett, Lonny. *Nourishing Destiny: The Inner Tradition of Chinese Medicine.* 1st ed. Massachusetts: Spirit Path Press, 1999.

Jung, Carl. *Memories, Dreams, and Reflections: An Autobiography.* London: Harper Collins, 1967.

Mate, Gabor. *When the Body Says No: The Cost of Hidden Stress.* New Jersey: Wiley, 2011.

Pressfield, Steve. *Do The Work: Overcome Resistance and Get Out of Your Own Way.* New York: Black Irish Entertainment, 2011.

Pressfield, Steven. *Turning Pro: Tap Your Inner Power and Create Your Life's Work.* New York: Black Irish Entertainment, 2012.

Sparks, J. Gary. *At The Heart of Matter: Synchronicity and Jung's Spiritual Testament.* Toronto: Inner City books, 2007.

Sparks, J. Gary. The *Call of Destiny: An Introduction to Jung's Major Works.* Toronto: Inner City Books, 2023.

Notes

THE BEGINNING: THE INTRODUCTION

1   Hollis, *Finding Meaning in the Second Half*, p. 31

2   Jarrett, *Deepening Perspectives*

3   Jarrett, *Deepening Perspectives*, p. 23

THE ADAPTATIONS: NECESSARY AND DESTRUCTIVE

4   Hollis, *Finding Meaning in the Second Half*, p. 63

5   Hollis, *Finding Meaning in the Second Half*, p. 63

6   Hollis, *Finding Meaning in the Second Half*, p. 67

THE STORY: PERSONAL PAST AND BEING SPECIAL

7   Jarrett, *Deepening Perspectives*

8   Jarrett, *Deepening Perspectives*, p.31

THE REASONS: NEEDING MORE TIME

9   Jarrett, *Deepening Perspectives*, p.23

10   Gracie, *Breathe*, p. 86

11   Pressfield, *The War of Art*, p. 48.

12   Jarrett, *Deepening Perspectives*, p. 24

13   Jarrett, *Deepening Perspectives*, p. 24

THE CALL: THE UNCONSCIOUS

14   Hollis, *Finding Meaning in the Second Half*, p. 253

15   Jung, *Analytical Psychology*, p.5.

16   Rubin, *The Creative Act*, p. 400

17   Hollis, *Finding Meaning.* Quoting Jung, *Psychological reflections*, p. 334

18   Johnson, *Inner Work*, p. 75

19   Carroll, *Something Deeply Hidden*, p. 16

THE RESPONSIBILITY: THE DUTY

20   Jarrett, *Deepening Perspectives,* p. 20

21   Hollis, *Finding Meaning,* p. 65 quoting Franz Kafka letters

22   Rubin, *The Creative Act,* p. 300

23   Jung, *Analytical Psychology,* P. 85-87

24   Johnson, *Inner Work,* p. 191

25   Rubin, *The Creative Act,* p. 333

THE CHALLENGE: THE TRAINING

26   Jarrett, *Deepening Perspectives,* p. 18

27   Rubin, *The Creative Act,* p. 389

28   Rubin, *The Creative Act,* p. 274

THE DECISION: THE SHIFT

29   Jarrett, *Deepening Perspectives,* . p78

30   Jarrett, *Deepening Perspectives,* . p78

31   Pressfield, *The War of Art,* p. 48

32   Jarrett, *Deepening Perspectives,* . p63

33   Jarrett, *Deepening Perspectives,* . p12

34   Jarrett, *Deepening Perspectives,* . p17

About the Author

A. Bisset is a friend to all dogs, a writer, and lover of mixed martial arts. Professionally speaking she has degrees in Psychology and Chinese Medicine and runs an acupuncture practice. She is continuing personal education in Quantum Physics and Jungian Analysis as well as spending time with friends and family and living a good life. You can write her at abissetwriter@gmail.com with questions, concerns, compliments or secrets.

www.ingramcontent.com/pod-product-compliance
Lightning Source LLC
Chambersburg PA
CBHW031326250726
48656CB00005B/1994